ROBIN A
I0051878
THE RA REPORT
Bankable Business Nuggets
For the Rising Entrepreneur

ISBN:
ISBN-13: 978-0-9980936-1-1

Digital Photo Illustration

Maclean Adu/@ClingArt

Artwork | Book Design | Layout

Emkron Studios | Phoenix White

TABLE OF CONTENTS

MY OBSERVATION

There's something fascinating about surrounding yourself with successful business people. I've done it for years, even before considering going into business for myself. For a long time, I was in the position of an executive assistant to a few high-profile people, and because I was the right-hand, I was always in "the room". In my opinion, "the room" means any coveted location at any time where insiders or prominent people meet up to converse, eat, or conduct business that the main public is not privy to.

There were many things for me to assess during those years. I observed how successful people walked, talked, excelled, made mistakes, lost money and regained it. I saw how they seemed to operate with business clues that only they knew about. I witnessed the inner workings of "outsiders" trying to get in the circle and what most of them did to fail, but I also witnessed how a select few were very successful in networking to get in.

One of the most important notes that I took away with me is the bravado and confidence that successful people obtained that accompanied them to their position in the marketplace.

Starting a business always has and always will begin with the belief in what you offer as a product or service; however, there are nuggets that I want to share that you can consider for yourself along your business journey. Whether you're an entrepreneur or a corporate individual looking to get promoted in your line of work, these tips will be helpful to keep in the back of your mind.

It's imperative to know that positions, jobs, gigs, career moves, or whatever you wish to call them, are the least of your concerns. People put too much emphasis on the "thing" they're trying to attain, and not enough focus on true essence of the journey.

The essence, or the "je ne sais quoi" is hard to pin point. It's more to it than just a few tips or tricks to get in the door, but this guidebook is meant to help you open the possibilities for your own journey and in your own way.

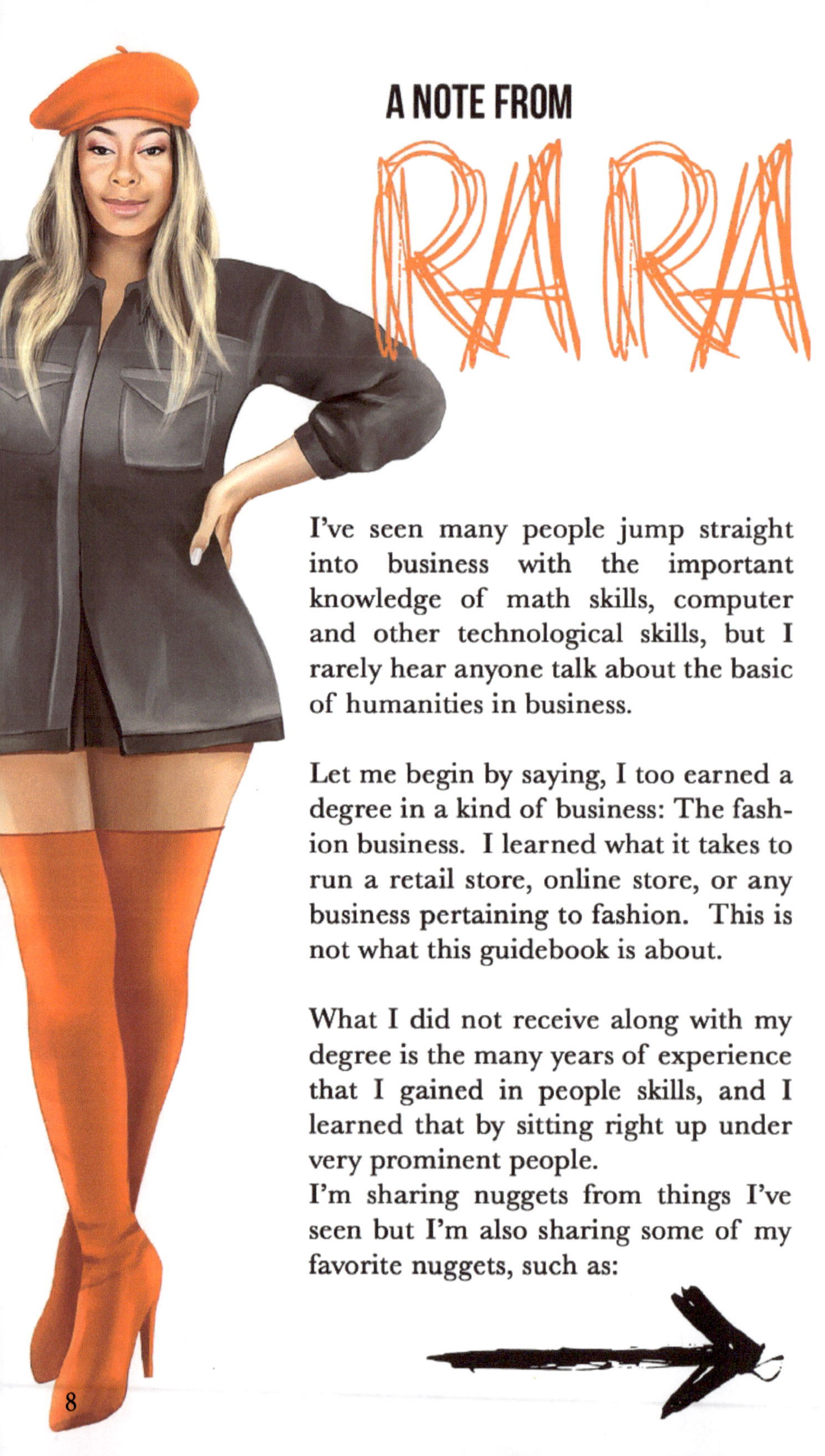

A NOTE FROM RA RA

I've seen many people jump straight into business with the important knowledge of math skills, computer and other technological skills, but I rarely hear anyone talk about the basic of humanities in business.

Let me begin by saying, I too earned a degree in a kind of business: The fashion business. I learned what it takes to run a retail store, online store, or any business pertaining to fashion. This is not what this guidebook is about.

What I did not receive along with my degree is the many years of experience that I gained in people skills, and I learned that by sitting right up under very prominent people.
I'm sharing nuggets from things I've seen but I'm also sharing some of my favorite nuggets, such as:

DONT BE INSECURE

Don't psyche yourself out of an opportunity because you think you're up against a seemingly perfect competitor. Even that competitor has an insecurity or weakness that you don't know about. You may be stronger and smarter, but you'll never know if you're afraid of competing.

Also,

Own up to your wrong doings. Apologize when necessary so that you remain in good standing. It's important to keep in mind that apologizing won't always fix your issues but it will at least make you a respectable person.

What you are about to read is a guide to help you remember that as a rising entrepreneur, some of the basics are sometimes the most important things to remember.
Enjoy!

Love,
RaRa

INNER VOICE

Recite these affirmations daily until you believe each one in the deepest part of your soul.

AFFIRMATION 1

"I'M NOT TOO OLD OR TOO YOUNG TO START A BUSINESS ENDEAVOR."

You can hold yourself back for years if you don't believe that as you stand, right here and now, you are more than capable of bringing your thoughts, creativity, and passions to life.

AFFIRMATION 2

"WHAT GOD HAS FOR ME IS INCAPABLE OF BEING STOPPED BY ANY PERSON, ANY FORCE, OR ANYTHING."

Don't get caught up in looking to your left and your right to see what other people have. You are in a lane all by yourself. What's coming to you is yours and no one else's.

"TODAY, I OVERCOME THE FEAR OF THE UNKNOWN. I DEFEAT THE RESISTANCE THAT COMES WITH WORKING TOWARDS MY GOALS."

Every time you have a desire to do something great, an unseen force in the form of procrastination, uncertainty, and even doubt tends to push back. Do something, even minor, towards your goal to combat this resistance.

AFFIRMATION 4

"I WILL DO GOOD THINGS TO SERVE HUMANITY WITH WHAT I BUILD."

The responsibility for owning a business or creating a successful life is making sure to give back by serving humanity, whether it's hiring people, donating goods or services, or using your earnings to serve others. You will be rewarded for doing good things with what you build.

AFFIRMATION 5

"I DESERVE TO HAVE WHAT I BELIEVE I CAN HAVE AND WHAT I WORK HARD FOR."

It's a law…believe that you can have it, speak it out loud, work for it, and you will receive it.

THE
RISE

RARA'S NUGGET

Know - It - All

No one likes a "know-it-all". Be teachable, approachable and open to learn.

RISE 1

Get Dressed

Get up every day and get dressed like you've got somewhere to go. It creates an effect in your mind of purpose and forward movement. When you move with intention, you will draw that type of positivity towards you.

RISE 2

Come Correct

Know exactly what you want or need and hold off on approaching anyone about it unless you can convey it clearly. Otherwise, you may play your favor card too soon.

RISE 3

Know The Players

"Always know the players before you get to the table." -Sonja Norwood

Complete thorough research before taking any meetings with anyone. Once you know who and what you're dealing with, you can be better prepared.

RISE 4

Be Aware of Your Brand

Google yourself, look up your name on hashtags, and even ask around. What do people say about you? No one should be able to bring up something against you that you don't already know. If there is something that doesn't look too good, be prepared to either explain it, apologize for it, or have a strategy behind it.

RISE 5

Confidence is Major

Act like you've been there before. No one knows if you're inexperienced or not unless you tell them so. Confidence and not haughtiness, is the key. Confidence is a strength and attractive. Arrogance is weakness and unappealing.

RISE 6

Name Dropping

Be 100% certain that by using an individual's name to get your foot in the door, it will gain you leverage instead of harming you because of your association.

Some people may have a disguised reputation that you know nothing about.

RISE 7

Treat Everyone Like The CEO

If you ever walk into an establishment and see someone mopping the floor, always treat that person with the same respect as you would the CEO. There are plenty of people who miss out on opportunities because they rudely address the person cleaning, thinking it's the janitor, when in fact, he or she was the CEO after all.

RISE 8

Point of Reference

A great tip for introducing yourself to someone you'd like to work with or get to know:

When you meet a person the first time, introduce yourself and make small talk but don't be too hard-pressed to exchange contact information with them unless there is truly a mutual interest there.

Wait until the next time you see them again. Re-introduce yourself and offer the point of reference to where you met the first time. This will establish comfort and a sense of trust for them.

RISE 9

Be Prepared

It's a good idea to have your business in order first before trying to network or collaborate with someone. (Website, DBA, business bank account, business phone line, etc.)

Have some type of establishment beforehand so when people research you and your business, you're already several steps ahead.

RISE 10
Opportunity vs. Opportunist

Don't be an opportunist. People can smell them from miles away. This is usually the person who's looking for a quick come up from nearly everyone they meet, and it usually only benefits them. Instead, look for opportunities that tend to have multiple benefits for people other than yourself.

RARA'S NUGGET

Use Your Strengths

What are your strengths? List them out. Use your strengths to get you a foot in the door.

Don't focus on your weaknesses unless you're reflecting in your private time.

THE
GRIND

RARA'S NUGGET

Travel

Travel as much as you can.
The world is full of amazing new things and people. Opportunities to expand your business and brand are far beyond the five-mile radius in which you live.

GRIND 1

Don't Forget

Once you secure a seat at the table, don't forget who invited you to eat.

You don't have to be indebted to anyone necessarily, but never forget who helped you get to the table. This also includes business endeavors. Don't get to a prominent place of success or fame and forget your initial supporters, customers, and followers. Remember anyone who helped get your business off the ground.

GRIND 2

Be Fair to Yourself

Beyoncé said it best! "Being polite and business don't match."

There's nothing wrong with being nice to people but don't allow anyone take your kindness for weakness either. Often, you'll need to learn the power of thickening your skin and getting straight to the point. Teach people how to treat you and they will follow suit.

GRIND 3

Play your Cards Right

Don't ask for favors based on unplanned or half thought out ideas. Make sure that it's properly mapped out and intentional. If you utilize a favor and it flops, people are less likely to be forgiving next time you ask.

Be smart about the cards you play. Don't just ask for everything, because when you need an important favor you may have already blown your opportunity.

GRIND 4

Ask For What You Want

Ask for what you want, not what you think they'll give you. Do you need a loan? Do you need sponsorship or donations? How will you get what you require if no one knows exactly what you want or need? The biggest mistake you can make is underestimating yourself, your talent or your product or service.

If you've ever heard the motto, "closed mouths don't get fed", that's what this means. Your request is more respectable when it's real, straightforward, and unapologetic.

GRIND 5

"Say Yes"

If an opportunity presents itself, you may not know how to do the job, but my rule is:

If it doesn't harm you or your family and it resonates in your spirit, then say "yes" and learn along the way. Opportunity favors those who are willing.

GRIND 6

Don't Allow Anyone to Taint Your Vision

Your vision is the most important thing you have. It belongs to you only. Be careful to only allow those you trust inside of your vision.

GRIND 7

Practice Makes Perfect

Fear often holds you hostage from making any moves because of too much practice in our minds. Seeing the vision in your mind vs. seeing it in real life are two different things.

How often do you say to yourself that you'll practice at home or silently in your mind before you put real action behind what you're saying? Probably quite often.

You will never perfect things until you begin to practice what you're thinking in real life.

GRIND 8

Get Out of Your Feelings

Put your feelings to the side when you're dealing in business. Assume that everyone you deal with is just as busy as you are. That means if they are snappy, rude, or emotional, it may have nothing to do with you. Get out of your feelings or it could mess up potential business.

GRIND 9

Watch Yourself

In your entrepreneurial endeavor, never get too comfortable. Someone is always coveting your position. Don't take your relationships or position for granted. Never fall into the mindset that you're safe just because you "know" someone. If you're slacking on the job but trying to rely solely on your connections, someone else might sneak up and take your position.

GRIND 10

Watch Your Word

A person's word is their invisible debit card. Every time you make a promise or commitment, it's like swiping the card and what you say, either withdraws from or deposits into your bank of trust. Sadly, people will still be around you or conduct business with you without you knowing where your account stands with him.

If you have a history of broken lies or promises, your account may be permanently overdrawn, and you won't be able to mend the relationships you have.

RARA'S NUGGET

Relax

Give yourself permission to kick your feet up and relax when you should. Taking time to breathe is just as important as the grind work that you put in. If you are uptight, restless, or sleepy, it's easy to overlook the important day-to-day details in business or work. In addition, there's no way to be at your best if you're not feeling your best. Relaxation is pivotal to your success.

Try one day per week. If that's too much, start with an hour per day.

SECURE

RARA'S NUGGET

Be Ethical

Securing the bag should never come by stepping on anyone's toes to do so. Also, as you begin to grow, you'll see opportunities that may benefit someone else instead of you. Don't be afraid to pass along business, opportunities, and even money to other people on the rise.

Deposit more than you withdraw. You're more valuable to people when you keep adding to their lives. Deposit so much value into their lives that when it's time for you to ask of them, it will be hard to turn you down.

SECURE 1

Start From The Bottom

Learn to do every aspect of your job yourself. When you hire someone, you want to know exactly what their job entails in case you're ever in a position where you must be hands on.

As an entrepreneur, you should be able to take on any aspect of running your business at any given point.

SECURE 2

$1Million Connection

Your network or contact list can often be more valuable than money itself. The truth is, you can be poor in cash but have an amazing lifestyle based on who you know. Treat everyone with the utmost respect as though they were each worth 1 million dollars or more.

SECURE 3

Put Everything On Paper

Even the best people with the best intentions go back on their word and sometimes it's just that they forgot what they've said. Write it down. Many have learned lessons and made plenty of mistakes not having agreements drawn up. At some point you can have an attorney draw one up for you, but don't underestimate the power of searching for templates online for what you need.

When utilizing templates online, you can still modify it to your exact needs.

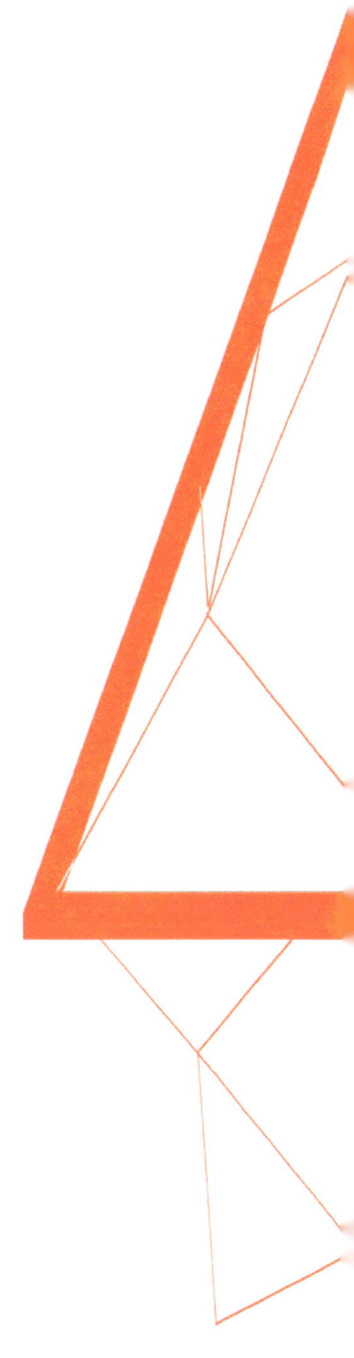

SECURE 4

Be Humble

Never assume you've already secured the bag and start slacking on insignificant details due to your certainty about landing new business. Treat each opportunity, new customer or client like it's brand new to you, each time.

Be humble and be grateful and people will likely want to do business with you again.

SECURE 5

Keep Your Name Great

Even if someone is baiting you to bad mouth someone else, don't fall for the trap. It's never a good idea to bond over negativity of another person. Two things: the word usually gets back around, and it speaks volumes of your character to the person you're speaking with. By you speaking negatively about someone else, it only shows them that you could possibly do the same to them one day.

SECURE 6

Get Your Own Business

Don't go after anyone else's customers, clients or partners. It may seem enticing but in the long run, you'll look shady for doing it. The world of business is very small. You don't want to gain a bad reputation, and the fact of the matter is that there are more than enough potential customers to go around.

SECURE 7

Send Written "Thank You" Letters

Say thank you. You'll immediately stand out above the rest. The art of thoughtfulness seems to have gotten lost in this generation. Find correct spelling of names, double check the spelling on notes, emails, and letters.

You'd be surprised at how many people feel entitled when doing business with others but saying "thank you" let's people know that you sincerely appreciate their time and deeds.

SECURE 8

Invest Wisely

We're all investing something every single day. We invest our time, money and other commodities. Make sure that you invest in yourself.

Equipment, knowledge, workshops, conferences and books are great options. Do what's necessary to add value to yourself first, your family, and then your business.

SECURE 9

Use Your Strong Voice

If you sound shaky and unsure when conducting business, you sound untrustworthy and new to the game. No one wants to feel like they're dealing with amateurs so, speak up!

SECURE 10

Don't Overprice

Don't overprice based on who you think people are or what kind of money you believe they have. The correct way is to be fair and get the business. Hopefully you will build a long-standing relationship, experience and value, and then your compensation will also rise because of it.

RARA'S NUGGET

Put Yourself On The Map

As much as you can, try to make every bit of progress pertaining to your own career or journey that you can. If you work hard enough and you're persistent, the right people will see you at the right time and want to connect and collaborate with you.

About the Author

Robin Ayers is an Entertainment Host, Author and Speaker. Her first self-published book, "Unspoken Languages: Making Your Beliefs Speak for You," was released in 2016.

In addition to her growing business as an adult, many young adult years were spent as an executive assistant to several high-profile individuals, to whom Robin played a pivotal role. As the "right hand" and liaison through many business deals, she was able to attain knowledge of what goes on behind the scenes in top secret business meetings.

Learning certain behaviors and do's and don'ts of many established business people, Robin wanted to give the basic tips for the growing entrepreneurial millennials on the rise. Even sharing some of her favorite "nuggets" such as "Don't be insecure," and "Apologize."

THANK YOU

A few influential people that I need to thank:

Beverly Peele:
American Supermodel and Actress

Thank you, Bev, for taking me under your wing at an impressionable age. Being a Supermodel and a businesswoman, and by taking me in as your personal assistant, you opened the world up to me. Thank you for showing me confidence, grace, and how to value myself.

Dawn Haynes:
Business Owner/Philanthropist

Dawn, I had never seen anyone own and operate a fulltime business like you. You taught me that it was mandatory to be treated with respect. You showed me what it was like to do business with high profile clients and maintain a friendship with them at the same time. I paid attention to your business savvy and how to plan five steps ahead. Thank you for giving me gems to take with me on a lifetime journey.

Sonja Norwood:

Artist Manager/Businesswoman

I would really like to thank you for allowing me to "sit at your feet" and gain wisdom from your extensive knowledge in the entertainment business. I love your ability to treat everyone with the same respect, regardless of their status. You taught me to protect myself, my business, and those in my immediate circle. You also taught me the art of being on top of my business from breaking down contracts to preparation for meetings. You educated me then trusted me to fly. You allowed me to flop at times and you'd pick me right back up, dust me off and set me up for success again. I appreciate your on-going conversations and teachable moments from the bottom of my heart.

Ray J:

Businessman/Artist

You identified my potential and without even realizing it, you positioned me perfectly in sight to watch you work. From you, I learned finesse, professionalism, and 100% pure, unadulterated hustle. You know how to make money but even more impressive, how to make sure your team makes money. Thank you for reminding me that being a likable person will also help you in business dealings.

Cash Jones:

Businessman/Artist Manager

One of the most influential people that came into my life to show me how to be street smart in business. You showed me up-close and personal the art of leveraging one thing for another and how to gain the most from every opportunity. Thank you for listening and answering every question that I had, big or small. You are the epitome of "putting yourself on the map".

www.ingramcontent.com/pod-product-compliance
Lightning Source LLC
Chambersburg PA
CBHW041716200326
41519CB00005B/277